Let's Talk About Heaven

Debby Anderson

CVP

Chariot Victor Publishing
A Division of Cook Communications

A Note to Parents

Because of the simplicity of children and the complexity of this subject, I have simplified terms and times, using the name "heaven" to describe all of the eternal state of believers. Feel free to answer a child's questions with, "I don't know, yet . . . but God knows. He has the very best planned for us."

My desire for all children who read this book, and for their parents, is that they experience a sense of anticipation, security, and worshipful wonder as they think about our future home.

—D.A.

Acknowledgments

Baker, Don. *Heaven*. Portland, Oregon: Multnomah Press, 1983.
Bayly, Joseph. *Heaven*. Elgin, Illinois: David C. Cook Publishing Co. 1977.

Chariot Victor Publishing
A division of Cook Communications, Colorado Springs, Colorado 80918
Cook Communications, Paris, Ontario
Kingsway Communications, Eastbourne, England

LET'S TALK ABOUT HEAVEN
© 1998, 1991 by Debby Anderson for text and illustrations

Designed by Donna Nelson
First printing, 1991
Printed in the United States of America
02 01   Year/Printing 15 14 13 12 11 10 9

Unless otherwise indicated, all Scripture quotations in this publication are from the *Holy Bible, New International Version*®. Copyright © 1973, 1978, 1984, International Bible Society. Used by permission of Zondervan Publishing House. All rights reserved.

Verses marked (TLB) are taken from *The Living Bible* © 1971, owned by assignment by the Illinois Regional Bank N.A. (as trustee). Used by permission of Tyndale House Publishers Inc., Wheaton, IL 60189. All rights reserved.

Library of Congress Cataloging-in-Publication Data

Anderson, Debby
    Let's talk about Heaven/Debby Anderson
  p. cm.
  Summary: Simple text and Bible verses answer questions about Heaven.
  ISBN 0-78143-077-1
    1. Heaven—Christianity—Juvenile literature.
  [1. Heaven. 2. Christian Life.] I. title
  BT 849.A53 1991
    236'.24-dc20   91-312
                               CIP
                               AC

I will come and do for you all the good things I have
promised, and bring you home again. For I know the
plans I have for you, says the Lord. They are plans for
good and not for evil, to give you a future and a hope.

Jeremiah 29:10-11 (TLB)

Dedicated to Joseph and Mary Lou Bayly,
whose compassion, humor, and
understanding inspired this book.

With appreciation to Pastor Lee and Karen Carpenter,
Homer and Betty Ostien,
Dr. Carl Pfeil, and Maisie Van Doren.

Do not let your hearts be troubled….In my Father's house are many rooms; … I am going there to prepare a place for you. And if I go and prepare a place for you, I will come back and take you to be with me….

John 14:1-3

Have you ever wondered what heaven will be like? Someday—in the twinkling of an eye—we're going there! It will be our forever home. But we all have lots of questions about it. Some of those questions God has already answered in His book, the Bible.

First of all...
Who is going to be

Every person who is in God's family! Because Jesus rose from the dead and lives forever, we can, too! We need to ask Jesus to forgive our sins—the bad things we think and say and do. Next we need to thank Him for dying on the cross for us. Right then, God makes us part of His family.

"I'll get to see my grandpa who died. I miss fishing with him."

"I told my friend at school about Jesus, and he decided to join God's family, too. I'm glad we'll still be friends in heaven!"

"I wish I could play with my baby sister. She died before I could even see her, but I'll get to know her in heaven!"

6

in heaven?

Konitchiwá!
(Japanese)

Buenas Dias!
(Latin America)

Visashóom!
(India)

Shalom!
(Hebrew)

Sawubóna!
(Zulu, S. Africa)

God's forever family will be filled with friends from every nation, tribe, people, and language. We will all belong to each other.

Salaam Allekóom!
(Arabic)

Howdy!
(U.S.A.)

Ciao!
(Italy)

7

Our favorite Bible story characters will be in God's forever family. What would you like to ask them?

The boy who gave his lunch

Queen Esther

The Wise Men

Samson

Daniel

Cornelius the centurion

Noah and his wife
"How did the animals know to come?"

Since we will be living together as a family, we will all know and love each other just as God knows and loves us. God will call each of us by name.

Dorcas
"Can you teach me to sew?"

Naaman's servant girl
"What's your name?"

Peter
"Can Dad and I go fishing with you?"

Zacchaeus

9

What will I be like

You will be yourself—one of a kind—but you'll be *perfect*. Wow! How God will do this is still a secret. We aren't ready to understand just yet.

Everything will be:

There will be no:

OLD

sadness

lying

thirst

evil

badness

crying

pain

dying

grumpiness

fear

hunger

darkness

shyness

night

NEW

safe

thankful

clean

strong

light

bright

honest

good

alive

happy

healthy

forgiven

If you're shy now, you'll feel right at home in heaven. If you're sad now, you'll laugh in heaven. God Himself will wipe away your tears … forever.

10

in heaven?

God will give us a new kind of body. We will be able to explore everything about our new home.

The blind will see.

The weak will walk ... run ... dance! (No wheelchairs in heaven!)

The deaf will hear.

The slow will understand.

We'll be able to run and never get tired... uphill or down!

God will also give the animals
a new way of life. Even now,
all creation is waiting to be free.
What will this freedom be like?

The wolf will live with the lamb,
the leopard will lie down with the goat,
the calf and the lion and the yearling together;
and a little child will lead them.
The cow will feed with the bear,
their young will lie down together,
and the lion will eat straw like the ox….
for the earth will be full of the knowledge
of the Lord as the waters cover the sea.

Isaiah 11:6-9

13

Which animal do you want to play with first?

Don't you wonder if
animals will talk?

What color are
dinosaurs?
Why did they
become extinct?

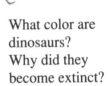

Where did You get the idea for the platypus?
Is he made of spare parts?

Do anteaters like strawberry ice cream? Vanilla?

Are ten-foot tigers ticklish?

We all wonder about our pets. We can trust our kind God to do what is the very best for them. He knows when even a tiny sparrow falls to the ground.

What will our forever home be like?

No eye has seen, no ear has heard, no mind has conceived what God has prepared for those who love Him.

I Corinthinans 2:9

Right this very second, Jesus is getting a wonderful place ready for each one of us. He has the very best planned. He knows that it's best to keep most of it a surprise . . . but we can *imagine* what it might be like!

Sarah hopes for sunny windows.

Kyle wants bunk beds—
for playing, not sleeping!

16

Jenny imagines "cotton candy clouds that we can eat, with berries in them. Maybe God will give us the recipe!"

Joey likes horses, cows, and frogs.

Melissa hopes for a sky-blue room with real live teddy bears.

Andrew wants watermelon and strawberries.

What do you imagine you'll find in heaven?

Tim hopes for a rocket ship.

Maybe you're right! But let's see what God's book, the Bible, tells us for sure....

17

Part of our forever home is like a city . . . more beautiful than we could ever imagine or draw . . . bright as a jewel . . . clear as crystal . . . made of pure gold! The golden street is shinier than a new penny!

Our forever home doesn't need the sun or moon. Jesus' smiling love will be heaven's sunshine.

A tall wall of green jasper jewels surrounds the city. Its twelve foundations are layers of twelve different kinds of rich stones in all the colors of the rainbow:

chrysoprase

amethyst   jacinth   topaz

emerald   chalcedony

chrysolite   jasper   carnelian

sapphire   sardonyx

beryl

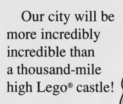

Our city will be more incredibly incredible than a thousand-mile high Lego® castle!

The wall has twelve gates, three in each direction—North, South, East, West—to welcome people from each corner of our wide world. Each gate is made of a single pearl, and at each stands an angel. The gates are always open.

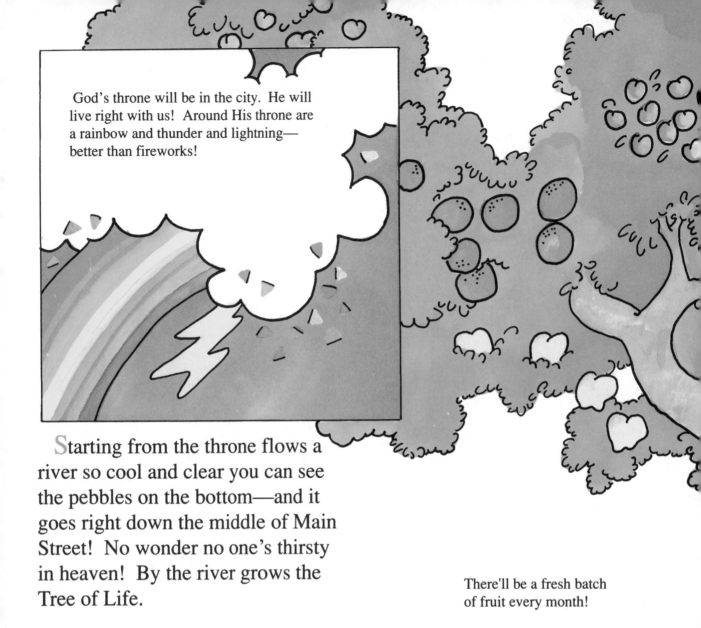

God's throne will be in the city. He will live right with us! Around His throne are a rainbow and thunder and lightning—better than fireworks!

Starting from the throne flows a river so cool and clear you can see the pebbles on the bottom—and it goes right down the middle of Main Street! No wonder no one's thirsty in heaven! By the river grows the Tree of Life.

There'll be a fresh batch of fruit every month!

And there's more—
more than words can tell!

Get ready,
universe....
Here we come!

21

But what will we do

The Bible only tells us a little, because we can understand just a little. It's God's surprise! For sure we will:

Worship

Together we will praise and thank God in music, in song … in everything we do!

Reign

We will be like princes and princesses in His Kingdom. As a gift, God will give us royal crowns. These crowns will be our gifts to give back to Him.

heaven?

We'll have to use a picnic table so long it would be listed in *The Guinness Book of Records!*

Fellowship

God's love will shine in our love for each other. We'll know each other. We'll belong together. We'll eat meals together.

Learn

Here on earth, one way to get to know God is by studying His creation. In our forever home, we will have all the time and tools we need to discover, to explore, to experiment, to create, to design.

Serve

To show God our thankfulness, we'll all help … and we'll enjoy every minute of it!

Rest

Nobody will need to hurry or worry… just enjoy.

28

Maybe we will:

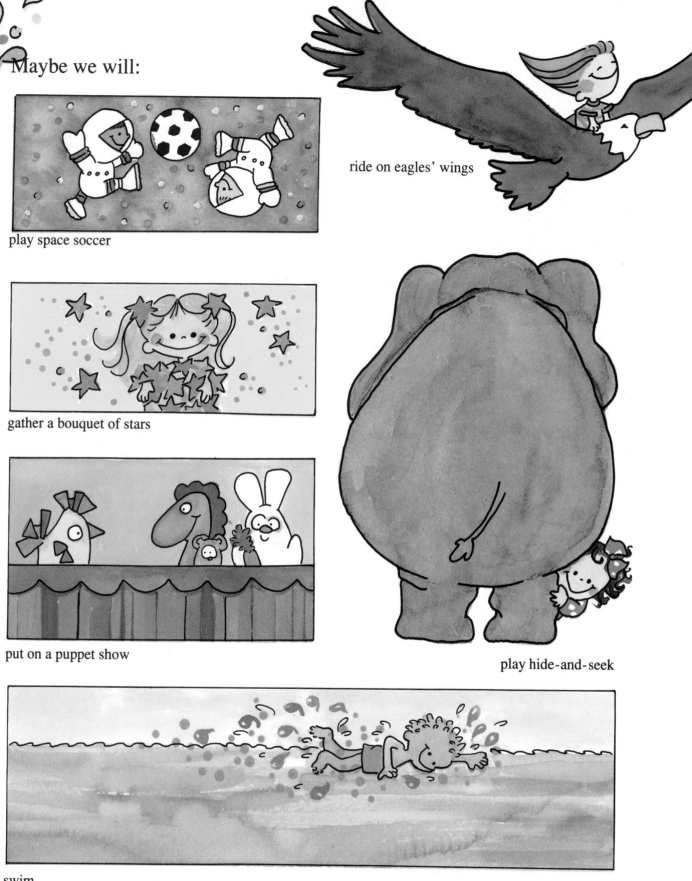

play space soccer

ride on eagles' wings

gather a bouquet of stars

put on a puppet show

play hide-and-seek

swim

27

We've learned quite a bit, but you may have even *more* questions about heaven, like:

What is Grandma doing in heaven right now? (Probably helping to get things ready!)

What do angels look like?

Is there a sandbox?

Will we fly?

Will we live in houses or apartments or cabins—or something we've never heard of before?

We do know for sure that God loves us. He has the very best planned for us. He is filling our forever home full of fantastic surprises that we can't even imagine or understand right now!

And we do know for sure what the *best* part of heaven is. . . .

29

It's being home with Jesus! *Forever,* we will talk and laugh and hug each other and say, "I love you." *Forever,* we will worship Him in everything we do. *Forever,* we will live in the light of His love.

Heaven is being home with Jesus.

30

Psalm 23

The Lord is my shepherd, I shall not be in want.
He makes me lie down in green pastures,
he leads me beside quiet waters,
he restores my soul.
He guides me in paths of righteousness
for his name's sake.
Even though I walk through the
valley of the shadow of death,
I will fear no evil, for you are with me;
your rod and your staff, they comfort me.
You prepare a table before me
in the presence of my enemies.
You anoint my head with oil; my cup overflows.
Surely goodness and love will follow
me all the days of my life, and I
will dwell in the house of the Lord forever.

Index of Scriptural References